Bygone Edinburgh

Kevin McCormack

Ian Allan
PUBLISHING

Introduction

Edinburgh is a city which conjures up many different images: capital of Scotland, World Heritage Site, the Scottish Parliament, 'Athens of the North' (a reference to its numerous Grecian-style structures), 'Auld Reekie' (reflecting more smoky times), the Edinburgh Festival, Hogmanay (New Year) celebrations in Princes Street, etc. For me, it was my birthplace and where I lived briefly and spent many holidays in my childhood and youth. This book aims to capture, through the medium of colour photographs of transport, the atmosphere of Edinburgh as I remember it in the 1950s and '60s.

Readers of my numerous transport books, which have centred almost entirely on London, may be surprised to see my name associated with a book on Edinburgh. However, I do have Edinburgh credentials. My maternal grandmother, born Margaret Millar and raised in Gogar, on the western outskirts of Edinburgh, was in domestic service in the city for much of her life. I was born at 10 Royal Crescent in December 1946 but left three weeks later for Ealing, in West London. For some reason we moved to Edinburgh in 1952, living to the west of the city at Kingsknowe, but 10 months later we returned to Ealing — an expensive and disruptive exercise which will forever be a mystery to me.

I was very happy at Kingsknowe, which was where my love affair with steam engines began. Kingsknowe was served by the railway that ran from Carstairs (on the London–Glasgow main line) to Edinburgh's 'Caley' (pronounced 'Cally') station at the west end of Princes Street. We lived in a bungalow that overlooked the level crossing beside the railway station, and I spent many happy hours swinging on the gates (which opened horizontally, not vertically!), watching the trains go by (and driving my parents mad by refusing to come in for meals: "I'll be in after the next train" — and the next, and the next!). It might be the old 'Jumbo', No 57559, which often used to trundle past with a light goods train, or one of the Fairburn tanks (Nos 42268-73) that used to take me to school. We had no car, so it was a train to Merchiston followed by a bus journey to get me to George Watson's Boys' College.

I also lived in the vain hope of seeing a train on the seemingly disused Balerno branch nearby. My parents and I — and Springer spaniel 'Paddy' — would regularly follow the path down to the site of Hailes Halt and walk along the railway line, which wound its way above Colinton Dell and the Water of Leith. We would then enter the dark and dank Colinton Tunnel to Colinton station. I well remember the conversation: "Daddy, what happens if a train comes when we're in the tunnel?" "Don't worry, son, there are no trains on this line." "Daddy, if there are no trains, why aren't the lines rusty?" "I don't know!"

Just before we returned to London, in July 1953, my parents thought I would enjoy a visit to one of the Rosyth Naval Days at the dockyard across the Firth of Forth. I remember being taken aboard the aircraft carrier, HMS *Implacable*, and the destroyer, HMS *Aisne*, but I was not the slightest bit interested. Instead, I spotted a little steam engine, the dockyard shunter, rushed over to it and asked the driver if I could climb onto the footplate. There I stood in front of the blazing fire in absolute bliss, leaving my parents standing on the ground, trying unsuccessfully to entice me back to the ships!

Front cover: In 1962 Queen Victoria surveys the New Town from the top of the recently cleaned Royal Scottish Academy, as she has done since 1844, seven years after succeeding to the throne at the age of 18. Beyond is Sir Walter Scott's Gothic rocket ship, and in the distance Calton Hill: the Parthenon lookalike is the permanently unfinished National Monument commemorating the Napoleonic Wars, while the tower resembling an upended telescope commemorates Admiral Lord Nelson. In the foreground is brand-new Alexander-bodied Leyland Titan PD2, No 631. *Marcus Eavis*

Previous page: Subsequently famous for being the only preserved Edinburgh tram, car No 35, dating from 1948, stops outside Redford Barracks, Colinton. No 35 currently lives at the National Tramway Museum at Crich, near Matlock, Derbyshire, but, amazingly, is no longer the sole survivor. The body of a converted cable car, No 226, built in 1903 and withdrawn in 1938, became a holiday home, and the tram is now being restored by Lothian Buses. *Fred Yorke*

First published 2008

ISBN (10) 0 7110 3256 4
ISBN (13) 978 0 7110 3256 9

© Kevin McCormack 2008

Published by Ian Allan Publishing

an imprint of Ian Allan Publishing Ltd, Hersham, Surrey KT12 4RG
Printed in England by Ian Allan Printing Ltd, Hersham, Surrey KT12 4RG

Code: 0804/B

Visit the Ian Allan Publishing website at www.ianallanpublishing.com

For the next 12 years or so I visited
Edinburgh during most summer holidays
to visit my grandmother, before she came
to live with us in Ealing. Until the service
was withdrawn we would travel up the
East Coast main line from King's Cross to
Edinburgh Waverley on the steam-hauled
9.30am non-stop 'Elizabethan' express —
not for us the slower 10am 'Flying
Scotsman', which by that time stopped for
a crew change. The streamlined ex-London
& North Eastern Railway (LNER) 'A4'-
class steam locomotives (nicknamed
'Streaks') used on the 'Elizabethan' had
tenders (carrying the coal and water) fitted
with a small corridor, through which the
relief driver and fireman, who had been
resting in the first carriage, would walk at
the appropriate changeover time. In order
to see some different steam engines I once
suggested that we travel back from
Edinburgh via the Waverley route through
Hawick to Carlisle, then over the Settle &
Carlisle line and onwards to St Pancras —
awesome scenery, awful journey. It seemed
to take forever, and my mother said "Never
again!" The Waverley route north of the
border closed in 1969 (although there are
plans to reopen it), but the Settle & Carlisle
line survives.

With gas lamps still gracing George
Square, in the south of the city
(nowhere near George Street and the
New Town), the author's mother
stands outside her *alma mater*,
George Watson's Ladies' College, in
1962. The ladies have now joined the
boys in Colinton Road, and Edinburgh
University occupies these old school
buildings. *Author*

Before retiring to Morningside my grandmother had been in domestic service in Eildon Street, opposite the Royal Botanic Garden in Inverleith Row. If I was lucky I would see a goods train at the end of Eildon Street making its way to Granton Harbour. Our normal means of transport to 'Nana's' (she had a live-in position) was the route 23 tram and I have vivid — indeed scary — memories of descending The Mound as the tram lurched and squealed around the bends near the top. Although there were posts on the pavement, designed to stop a tram from leaving the tracks and falling onto the railway line that ran through Princes Street Gardens below, I couldn't see these posts being particularly effective in stopping a runaway tram.

I have many other recollections of Edinburgh in the 1950s and early 1960s: the cobbled streets with their aged gas lamps, many of which carried a date from around the 1870s; the ancient-looking Daimler buses of Edinburgh Corporation Transport (ECT), which often ran with their bonnet sides detached, presumably to reduce engine overheating; battling against what seemed like a hurricane in order to climb the Waverley Steps beside the North British Hotel; and the Co-Op's horse-drawn milk floats.

Besides road transport and steam trains, my interests included aircraft, but Turnhouse Airport (now Edinburgh International Airport) was a great disappointment. A World War 2 Spitfire guarded the RAF buildings, but there was little else to see. We used to visit Cramond and Dalmeny Woods for outings and admire the nearby Forth (railway) Bridge. The Forth road bridge did not open until 1964, so drivers of vehicles wishing to cross the Firth of Forth near Edinburgh had to catch the ferry that plied alongside the railway bridge. My grandmother often recounted seeing it under construction from the 'banking' beside Gogar railway station, next to her family's tiny cottage, before they moved to a new house nearby, 'Fairview' (now in the shadow of the Edinburgh City By-pass), where Grandpa Millar (my great grandfather) had a pig-farm and his own railway siding.

We had friends at the eastern end of the city, near Piershill, and I was always keen to visit them because they were close to that wonderful smoky hole, St Margaret's engine shed. Visitors had to be escorted because the main line bisected the depot and the foreman's office was on the opposite side of the line from our friends' house, but I was usually content to 'spot' the locomotives on the London Road side, where most of them stood and which could be reached 'unofficially' by scrambling down a bank.

We were normally in Edinburgh around Festival time, and a regular feature of these visits was attending the 'Searchlight' Tattoo on the Castle Esplanade, shivering under rugs (in August!). Princes Street was a magnet for shoppers, including my mother, but the only shop that interested me was the restaurant,

Mackies. The firing of the cannon at the Castle at 1pm was normally the signal to extract my mother from Smalls, the ladies' outfitters next door to Mackies, and have lunch.

Writing this book has been a nostalgic trip down memory lane. I am not familiar with the Edinburgh of today, although I know that, from a transport enthusiast's point of view, there are interesting times ahead with proposals to reintroduce trams, reopen the South Circular suburban railway line to passengers and build a second Forth road bridge. In the meantime Edinburgh continues to be one of the most popular cities in Europe for visitors, as evidenced by the increasing number of travellers using Edinburgh Airport all year round and, in particular, for the annual Edinburgh Festival, which has grown from strength to strength since its inception in 1947.

There has been much change since the photographs in this book were taken, mostly 40-50 years ago, although to a lesser extent in the city centre where conservation, sometimes lacking in the 1960s, has become an increasingly important priority. For those, of similar vintage to myself, who are familiar with bygone Edinburgh as well as for those too young to remember and for visitors less well acquainted with the city, I hope that the historic colour images featured in this book will be of interest, reflecting a more leisurely and dignified age. Some of the pictures were taken by my mother or myself, but the vast majority were taken by the following contributors, to whom I am most grateful: Fred Yorke (courtesy of the Scottish Tramway & Transport Society), Paul de Beer, Marcus Eavis, David Kelso, Bruce Jenkins, Ian Stewart, Maurice Bateman, Brian Patton, John Kaye, Peter Stubbs and Jim Oatway. Further thanks are due to Roger Jones for use of photographs taken by Jack Wyse and Frank Hunt, which are held by the Light Rail Transit Association (London Area), to Martin Jenkins for the use of images from the Online Transport Archive (which also now holds those of Maurice Eavis), and also to John May for his help. The intention has been to arrange the photographs geographically, starting at the Scott Monument in Princes Street and radiating around it from south to west, north and east, although a few exceptions to this principle have been made in the interests of colour matching.

Finally, if you spot yourself or your relatives in any of these photographs — and it has happened a few times with my books — you are welcome to write to me care of the Publisher.

Kevin R. McCormack
Ashtead, Surrey
January 2008

East and West Princes Street Gardens, as seen from the
Scott Monument in the mid-1950s. Trams still hold sway in
Princes Street, and two inter-town Bluebird coaches can be
seen making their way to the terminus at St Andrew
Square. The sunken railway line from Waverley station
curves round the base of the Castle rock in the left distance.
The distinctive building in the centre is the Royal Scottish
Academy, while, in the background, the long block
in Lothian Road, standing at the far end of the West
Gardens, is the Caledonian Hotel, fronting Princes Street
railway station. Several of the buildings in Princes Street
have since been demolished, including the prominent edifice
on the right belonging to the North British & Mercantile
Insurance Co, replaced by a BHS store.
Ian Stewart collection

Above: Edinburgh's principal station represents a further commemoration of the Edinburgh novelist and poet, Sir Walter Scott (1771-1832), being named after his 'Waverley' novels. Watched by a group of locospotters seated on a baggage trolley, two 'V2' mixed-traffic locomotives, Nos 60965 and 60813, stand at the western end in July 1959. Dominating the background and situated at the eastern end of Princes Street is the hotel (now known as the Balmoral) built in 1902 for the railway company which until 1923 operated out of Waverley station — the North British Railway (NBR). *Bruce Jenkins*

Right: A view from the Scott Monument of the west end of Waverley station, with a Class A3 Pacific locomotive heading a northbound train towards the Mound Tunnel. Although there has been a railway station in this area since 1846, the present station dates from the late 19th century, having been built in response to an increase in rail traffic generated by the opening in 1890 of the Forth Bridge. *David Kelso*

Left: About to enter the Mound Tunnel prior to arriving at Waverley station in May 1951 is 'A4' Pacific No 60024 *Kingfisher* (see also page 79). The locomotive is in British Railways' short-lived express-locomotive blue livery, which apparently failed to wear well and was replaced by green. The first carriage is still in LNER varnished teak. *Jack Wyse*

Below left: At the identical spot on the same day, blue-liveried 'A1' Pacific No 60161 (subsequently named *North British*) makes its way from Haymarket shed to Waverley station to haul a northbound express. None of this class of 50 locomotives survived into preservation, but one is currently being constructed, making it the first main-line steam locomotive to be built in Britain since 1960. *Jack Wyse*

Right: Yet another memorial to Sir Walter Scott was the naming of nearly 70 Scottish-based locomotives (Classes D29 and D30, as well as some 'D11s') after characters from his novels or poems. Here a member of the 'D30' ('Scott') class, No 62437 *Adam Woodcock* (a character from *The Abbot*), hauls a Waverley–Corstorphine local through Princes Street Gardens after emerging from the Mound Tunnel. *David Kelso*

Heading east along Princes Street close to the Scott Monument is an ancient-looking Metro-Cammell-bodied postwar Daimler bus, ECT No 117, which ran until 1962. Unlike many older types the Daimlers were not cosmetically modernised by the fitting of standardised glass-fibre fronts to disguise their age. On the right can be seen a British Railways lorry carrying a freight container for loading onto a railway flat wagon. *Brian Patton*

At the same location but turning from Princes Street into St David Street is ECT No 258, a traditional-looking Leyland PD2 of 1952 which lasted until 1970. In 1963 it was fitted with a glass-fibre front covering its external radiator, so that it more closely resembled the majority of the bus fleet. *Brian Patton*

In the late 1950s and early '60s some public transport operators, such as ECT, experimented with unpainted buses in the interests of economy. However, the unpainted vehicles quickly lost their shine and began to look scruffy. Leyland Titan PD2 No 795, built in 1957, pauses outside Littlewoods' store in Princes Street during July 1959, shortly before receiving conventional madder-and-white livery. Withdrawn in 1974, it became a playbus. *Bruce Jenkins*

In September 1956, with only two months of tramway operation remaining, car No 137, dating from 1935 and one of 84 domed-roof 'Standards' built by ECT between 1934 and 1950, pauses outside the uncleaned Royal Scottish Academy before climbing The Mound on a 23 working to Morningside station. *Bruce Jenkins*

In the Old Town, Leyland Titan PD2 No 471, in service from 1954 to 1975 and one of 300 tram-replacement buses with Metro-Cammell Orion bodywork, leads a Weymann-bodied Leyland Tiger Cub in the High Street, at its junction with George IV Bridge. Rising up behind the buses in this 1962 view is St Giles' Cathedral, parts of which reputedly date back to the 12th century. *Marcus Eavis*

A domed-roof 'Standard' tram negotiates the bends near the top of
The Mound. As described in the Introduction, descending at this point
was a death-defying experience, at least for a small boy! The safety posts
installed when electric trams were introduced in central Edinburgh
in 1924, augmented by some robust railings, were intended to prevent
a runaway tram from falling over the edge. The Mound, climbing up
to the Old Town, was man-made using surplus soil from the construction
of the New Town below, which commenced in 1767.
Paul de Beer / Online Transport Archive

Left: Princes Street is bustling in this view from 1966. At the centre of the picture is a rebodied ex-London Transport Guy Arab bus on a short working of route 31 to Edinburgh Zoo (instead of Corstorphine), while on the right is an attractive two-tone Austin taxicab.
Ian Stewart

Below: As once the Leyland Titans had replaced the trams, so the time came for the Titans themselves to be replaced. This view from October 1974 at the west end of Princes Street, opposite the Caledonian Hotel, portrays the transition. PD2 No 492, some 20 years old, is about to turn out of Princes Street into Lothian Road as a trio of Atlanteans, Nos 321 and 46 leading, head for Shandwick Place.
Marcus Eavis

An oversize load proceeds along Princes Street in this 1962 view of the New Town from the Argyll Battery at Edinburgh Castle. Built on volcanic rock, the Castle, once a mediæval military fortress, stands at the end of the Old Town's 'Royal Mile' leading to the Palace of Holyroodhouse.

Below the Castle rock was the Nor' Loch, drained in 1760 and now occupied by Princes Street Gardens, the railway line and Waverley station. *Marcus Eavis*

Catching up with Leyland PD2 No 631 in Princes Street, at the junction with Frederick Street, in January 1964 is a 1948-built Guy single-decker on learner duty. Withdrawn from passenger service in 1961 and as a driver-trainer in 1970, it is either No 839 (since preserved) or No 840 (less fortunate). The ornate lamp-standards, to which decorative lights have been attached, are a legacy of the tram era: traction poles in the centre of the road, rather than on either side of it, were a requirement in Princes Street to minimise the visual impact of the overhead wires. *Author*

Also in Princes Street and approaching the junction shown opposite is ECT No 204, one of only five Guy Arabs bought by ECT. Of 1949 vintage (and destined to be withdrawn in 1962), it has unusual bodywork by Northern Counties Motor & Engineering, the upper windows of the lower saloon being designed to improve vision for standing passengers. *Ian Stewart*

Bound for Edinburgh (Turnhouse) Airport, a virtually empty Duple-bodied Bedford coach dating from 1963 heads along George Street, approaching the junction with Frederick Street. Painted in ECT's black and white coach livery, it was to remain in the fleet for 10 years before being sold to a local school. The New Town's street network was laid out in a grid pattern (a smaller version of that in Milton Keynes, which is probably where the comparison ends!), and George Street was one of several roads running parallel with Princes Street. It was named after King George III, the reigning monarch when Parliament approved the expansion of the city in 1767, and was the principal street in the New Town. Neighbouring streets are also linked to royalty, *e.g.* Queen, Charlotte, Frederick, Hanover and, of course, Princes Street, named after the then Prince of Wales. *John Kaye*

A brand-new Leyland Titan PD2, No 607, stands at the west end of Princes Street, near the junction with Charlotte Street (from which another bus is emerging). One of a batch of 50 purchased by ECT in 1961/2, it was to remain in service until 1977. It carries illuminated advertising panels between the decks, a short-lived 1960s fad repeated elsewhere, notably in London, where a batch of Routemasters was so fitted. *John Kaye*

In another attempt to reduce painting costs ECT experimented with an all-red livery with gold lining on No 999, an Alexander-bodied Leyland PD3 of 1959. With Holy Trinity church in the background, this brand-new bus has just crossed the Telford-designed Dean Bridge over the Water of Leith and is about to terminate in Melville Street, in the West End. By 1962 ECT thought better of the idea, repainting the vehicle in traditional madder and white. *Bruce Jenkins*

Right: A Leyland Olympic coach on the airport service pulls out of George Street into Charlotte Street as a Daimler bus brings up the rear. Dating from 1951, the Olympic was originally a Leyland demonstrator and was in service in Edinburgh from 1952 to 1969, being converted from rear- to front-entrance in 1955. The large Fry's Chocolate advertisement, overlooking Charlotte Square, is necessarily dignified. A few products still bear the Fry's name today, despite the brand's now being owned by chocolate giant Cadbury's. *Bruce Jenkins collection*

Below: In the days before the Grouping of the railways into the 'Big Four' companies (in 1923) Scotland possessed several separate companies. The main company serving Edinburgh was the North British Railway, but the rival Caledonian Railway also had a presence, running into a terminus at the west end of Princes Street and operating some local lines. In this view from the summer of 1965 a Fairburn tank engine makes a spirited departure from Princes Street station. *Author*

Local people normally referred to Princes Street station as the 'Caley' (pronounced 'Cally'), not necessarily because of their knowledge of pre-Grouping railway companies but due to the Caledonian Hotel (built onto the front), construction of which started in 1903. This view from January 1964 depicts the concourse of the station, with its varnished-wood features. *Author*

In the late 1950s Edinburgh's local railway services were 'dieselised', although this intended efficiency failed to prevent passenger services such as that from Princes Street to Leith North from being withdrawn. In the final year of the line's public operation (1962) a diesel multiple-unit from Leith North passes the signalbox as it enters Princes Street station. Part of the trackbed leading to the station has been used for the Western Approach relief road, opened in 1974. *Marcus Eavis*

Above: Opened in 1870, Princes Street station closed on 6 September 1965, services being diverted into Waverley. On the last day a train is seen departing behind a neglected ex-London, Midland & Scottish Railway (LMS) Class 5 mixed-traffic locomotive, No 44954. A tired-looking water crane stands in the foreground. *Author*

Right: One of the last ex-Caledonian Railway locomotives to remain at Dalry Road shed, a mile down the line from Princes Street station, was this elegant Pickersgill Class 72, No 54478, dating from 1920. The class were nicknamed 'Caley bogies', and the last survivors ran until 1962, but, sadly, none was saved, although a relative of this type is preserved in Belgium. *Author's collection*

On 20 July 1961, seven months from withdrawal, NBR Class J83 No 68481 of 1901 shunts at Haymarket depot, beyond Edinburgh's West End. This picture reminds the author of a visit to Thornton, Fife, in 1960, when the driver of another 'J83', No 68459, which was shunting in the depot yard, beckoned him up into the cab and invited him to drive the locomotive back into the shed! The distance was only a few hundred yards, but it was a great thrill for a 13-year-old, illustrating the kindness often shown to young locospotters by railway staff in the days before Health & Safety considerations (and suspicion) predominated.
Jim Oatway

For 125 years St Cuthbert's Co-operative Society delivered milk in
Edinburgh by horse. The dairy was based in Fountainbridge, and the
stables were in nearby Grove Street. On the final day, 26 January 1985,
an empty milk-float on its way back to the stables heads along
Fountainbridge for the last time. *Peter Stubbs*

Left: In 1956 ECT No 480, from the first batch of tram-replacement Leyland PD2s, pauses in Home Street, adjacent to Tollcross tram depot, while a tram and a Morris taxicab pass by, heading northwards to the city centre. *Frank Hunt*

Above: One of the enduring tram-replacement Leyland PD2s, No 712 — a bus which gave 20 years' service, from 1956 to 1976 — approaches the railway bridge in Morningside Road in January 1972. Many considered these to be neat and attractive vehicles, but not so one city bailie (alderman), who described them, when they were first introduced, as 'ungainly, inelegant, monstrous masses of shivering tin'! *Author*

Left: When this view was recorded in 1962, almost 20 years before St Cuthbert's merged with Dalziel to become Scotmid, the horse-drawn milk-floats were rather more imposing. This one is pictured in Morningside Road, close to the Volunteer Arms ('Canny Man') public house, much patronised by the author's Uncle Gordon, who lived around the corner with his mother (the author's grandmother) in Canaan Lane. *Author*

Right: Around the corner in Canaan Lane, also in 1962, stands a splendid Rolls-Royce limousine, the car's red radiator badge denoting that it was built before 1931 (after which the badges were black). But, since it does not appear on the DVLA's vehicle-registration computer database, where is the car today? In the background is the tenement where the author's grandmother and two of her sisters had flats. *Author*

The Suburban & South Side Junction Railway opened in 1884, providing a circular route around the south of Edinburgh. Passenger services were withdrawn on 10 September 1962, but the line remains open to freight traffic, and there are proposals to reopen it to passengers. Reduced to hauling a freight train around the 'Sub' as a result of the creeping 'dieselisation' of express trains, 'A4' Pacific No 60002 *Sir Murrough Wilson* steams through Morningside Road station in 1962, to the delight of the author's mother, who, being 'well trained'(!), happened to have her camera ready. *Mrs E. J. McCormack*

The attractive flowerbed at Gorgie East, on the South Suburban railway line, two stations on from Morningside Road in a westerly direction (towards Haymarket), was symptomatic of the pride taken by many railwaymen at a time when most stations were still staffed. This scene dating from 8 September 1962 belies the fact that the station was to close two days later. *Author*

Above: The tram route to Colinton commenced operation in March 1926 and was converted to bus operation in October 1955. Close to the terminus, two wooden-bodied 'Standards' are about to pass in Colinton Road, between the grounds of Merchiston Castle School (on the left) and the Royal Artillery's Redford Barracks (right). Car No 268 dated from 1929. *Fred Yorke*

Right: Closed in 1943 when passenger services on the line from Edinburgh (Princes Street) to Balerno were withdrawn, the Caledonian Railway station at Colinton dated from 1874, when the line was opened, but was in a sorry state by the time this picture was taken in 1962. Freight services continued until 1967. (See also back cover.) *Author*

Turnhouse Aerodrome was built as a military airfield in 1915 and served as an RAF station until 1960, although civilian use was allowed. This view from August 1956 depicts two delta-winged Gloster Javelin fighters taking off from the old runway, which ran parallel to the Kirkliston Road. The Pentland Hills are in the background. Today's airport is in the distance on the right-hand side of the picture. First flown in 1951, the Javelin entered service with the RAF in 1956 and was withdrawn from operational duties in 1968. Ten still exist, but none is likely ever to fly again. *David Kelso*

In August 1956 a British European Airways (BEA) Viscount airliner, G-ANHA *Anthony Jenkinson*, is prepared on the apron at RAF Turnhouse for its return flight to London (Heathrow) Airport — providing the mechanic can fix the door! The Vickers Viscount, which made its first flight in 1948, was the world's first turbo-prop airliner to enter service, and BEA/British Airways operated the type from 1953 through to the 1980s. Nearly 450 were built, but only six (at most) remain in service today, all in Africa. *David Kelso*

Above: NBR Classes B and S, introduced in 1906 and 1914 respectively and later designated by the LNER as Classes J35 and J37, consisted of powerful little locomotives which undertook much of the freight work in the Edinburgh area. Seen at Saughton Junction, where the lines from Edinburgh to Glasgow and to the Forth Bridge diverge, 'J37' No 64623 returns a string of empty coal wagons from the industrial Forth–Clyde valley to the Lothian coalfields. *David Kelso*

Right: At Dalmeny Junction in August 1957, a Class B1 locomotive approaches Dalmeny station and the Forth Bridge with an Edinburgh–Perth train as a Class D49 'Shire' leaves the station with a Dundee–Edinburgh train. The Ochil Hills, in Fife, can be seen in the background. Completed in 1890, the bridge took seven years to build and involved some 5,000 workers, of whom up to 100 lost their lives in the process. *David Kelso*

Above: The Forth Bridge, nowadays more commonly known as the Forth rail bridge following the construction of the neighbouring road bridge, is pictured with two of the four vehicle ferries. It was (and still is) a formidable structure, intended to boost public confidence following the collapse in December 1879 of the Tay Bridge, which consigned a complete passenger train carrying 75 people to a watery grave (although the locomotive was recovered, repaired and returned to service). Earlier in 1879 construction had begun on a Forth Bridge designed by the engineer of the original Tay Bridge, but, not surprisingly, this was abandoned. Interestingly, it is no longer appropriate to refer to a seemingly never-ending job as being 'like painting the Forth Bridge', recent technological advances having produced longer-life paint which has freed the bridge from the permanent presence of painters. *Marcus Eavis*

Right: Sixteen days after its official opening on 4 September 1964, spectators admire the Forth road bridge, at that time the longest suspension bridge in Europe and the fourth-longest in the world. Nowadays the road vehicles seen here are probably of greater interest than the bridge, particularly as its cables are corroding, and it is due to be closed to heavy goods vehicles in 2013. An additional road crossing, either a tunnel or, more likely, another bridge, is optimistically planned for completion by this deadline. *Maurice Bateman*

Left: One of the ferries, decorated with bunting, stands at the South Queensferry quay, beside the Forth railway bridge, on the opening day of the road bridge, which is just visible in the mist behind the ship. *Mrs E. J. McCormack*

Above: Granton Square in the summer of 1974, populated by tram-replacement Leyland Titan PD2s (one on learner duty), by now nearly 20 years old. Beyond are Eastern Harbour and, on the right, the former hotel which is now HMS Claverhouse, a Royal Naval Reserve Sea Training Centre. *Marcus Eavis*

Left: A blue bus came to Edinburgh in April 1959, this Willowbrook-bodied Dennis Loline in Walsall Corporation livery spending a month demonstrating its potential, in exchange for an ECT vehicle. Walsall No 800, which had been exhibited at the 1958 Commercial Motor Show, stands at the Pilton terminus of route 19 while driver and conductress have a natter. *Brian Patton*

Below: Breaking the geographical sequence to travel eastwards beyond the ports of Granton, Newhaven and Leith, we reach Edinburgh's seaside resort, Portobello. Standing at the Town Hall terminus in April 1958 is a 1948-built Daimler bus, No 691. The demand for new buses in the immediate postwar period meant that, until new designs could be tried and tested, vehicles were still largely of prewar design, hence their archaic appearance. *Brian Patton*

While seven tram services terminated at the port of Granton, routes 23
and 27 terminated earlier, at Granton Road station, on the former
Caledonian Railway's branch from Princes Street station to Leith North.
The line closed to passengers on 28 April 1962, but the station building
was put to commercial use and survived until 1985. Car No 223 ran from
1939 until the end of tramway operation in November 1956.
Paul de Beer / Online Transport Archive

The port of Granton was where coal from the collieries around Edinburgh was brought by rail along the harbour branch for loading onto ships. The railway line was lifted in 1987 and is now a cycle path. Here car No 297, built in 1923 with open balconies on the upper deck (enclosed in 1930) has stopped short of Granton Square as a Hillman Minx speeds by. *Fred Yorke*

A streamlined tramcar dating from 1934/5 and a wooden-bodied 'Standard', No 104, dating from 1930 stand at Granton Square terminus. Middle Pier stretches into the distance on the left and a smart Austin Devon saloon stands on the right. The red container on the platform partition of No 104 is an honesty box for uncollected fares. *Fred Yorke*

Left: Pictured in the summer of 1974, ECT Leyland Titan PD2 No 711, by now in its 18th year of service, is well loaded as it stands outside HMS *Claverhouse* in Granton Square. The advertising on the side of the bus promoting long-distance flights by BOAC (British Overseas Airways Corporation) indicates that the merger with BEA to form British Airways has yet to happen. *Marcus Eavis*

Above: The transition from tram to bus was already in progress when this photograph was taken in Craighall Road, Newhaven. Route 11, from Stanley Road to Fairmilehead (not Joppa — the conductor is in the process of turning the blinds) was converted on 12 September 1956, while route 28 (Stanley Road–Braids) was one of the final two tram routes, running for the last time on 16 November 1956. Car No 88 gave 21 years of service following its construction in 1935. *Paul de Beer / Online Transport Archive*

Close to Granton Square, car No 48 stands in Lower Granton Road alongside the harbour railway line. Only six years old yet just two months from withdrawal (in November 1956), it is ready to depart for the Braid Hills. The author has disturbing memories of trying to play golf there in an ever-strengthening wind which turned out to be the tail end of Hurricane Hattie and which caused him and his mother literally to crawl back to the clubhouse, it being impossible to stand upright! *Bruce Jenkins*

Its aluminium finish shimmering in the sunshine, brand-new Leyland PD2 No 575 stands in Craighall Road, Newhaven, with the Firth of Forth and the hills of Fife stretching out beyond. Note that the bus is entirely devoid of paint, unlike No 795 (on page 12), which has acquired a madder (maroon) band. *Frank Hunt*

Left: The Stanley Road terminus of tram routes 7, 11 and 28 was moved in 1949 to the foot of Craighall Road, Newhaven, but the destination blinds were never altered, as apparent from this view of car No 262. Although ECT constructed most of its own trams, this vehicle, built in 1934, was one of 23 'Streamliners' purchased around this time from outside manufacturers, in this case English Electric. This car was another to put in 21 years of service. *Fred Yorke*

Above: In a distinctly period setting, car No 202, an early dome-roofed 'Standard' dating from 1935 (and yet another to clock up 21 years of service) turns the corner from Stanley Road into Newhaven Road in May 1955. Behind the tram, Whale Brae leads down to the old fishing port of Newhaven. *Paul de Beer / Online Transport Archive*

Left: Further east along the coast from Newhaven is Leith, Edinburgh's principal port and nowadays home to the Royal Yacht, *Britannia*. In the summer of 1974 a tram-replacement Leyland Titan PD2 on route 16 is seen on Bernard Street bridge, a relatively modern structure which replaced a remarkable swing bridge over the Water of Leith. A later Alexander-bodied PD2 on route 34 waits in the road called The Shore. *Marcus Eavis*

Above: Built in 1950 but of dated appearance, this Brockhouse-bodied Bristol L6B, No 771, stands at the terminus of route 1 in Easter Road, near Leith Central station, in September 1956, with just four more years of public service left. ECT bought only 15 of these Bristol buses, the order being placed before the manufacturer was nationalised in 1948 and debarred from supplying non-nationalised operators such as local authorities, apart from honouring existing orders. *Bruce Jenkins*

Above: Musselburgh, to the east of Leith, also had its own electric tramway system, running from Joppa to Port Seton. Edinburgh took over the line in 1932 and cut it back from Port Seton to Levenhall, where this shot was taken. Musselburgh racecourse can be seen on the left. Car No 367, dating from 1929, gave an impressive 26 years of service. *Fred Yorke*

Right: Another view at Levenhall, with a tram on route 21 ready to leave the terminus for the Post Office (or GPO, as it was usually called); located adjacent to the North British Hotel at the east end of Princes Street, the façades of this building have since been incorporated into the Waverleygate office development. Route 21 lost its trams in November 1954, but car No 81, built in 1933, found further use until September 1955. *Fred Yorke*

The first of a sequence of railway pictures taken at St Margaret's engine shed on 15 September 1965, this interior view depicts an historic veteran, Class J36 No 65243, built for the North British Railway in 1891. This locomotive served in France in World War 1, following which it was named *Maude* after Lt Gen Maude, Commander of British Forces in Mesopotamia. It then returned to normal life, finally being withdrawn from service in July 1966, whereupon it was preserved. It now resides on the Bo'ness & Kinneil Railway, to the west of Edinburgh. *Author*

St Margaret's motive power depot, situated near Piershill, was originally established in 1846 and closed in April 1967. Its function was to provide and service locomotives for local passenger and goods services, as opposed to Haymarket depot, on the other side of Waverley station, where express locomotives were based or serviced. In this view a somewhat over-powered local train hauled by Class B1 No 61344 passes a derailed diesel shunter. *Author*

Above: Bound for Waverley station on a passenger turn, ex-LMS Class 5MT No 45477 passes St Margaret's locomotive shed. According to its front buffer-beam the locomotive was based at Dalry Road, which depot served Edinburgh Princes Street station until the latter's closure on 6 September 1965 and which was itself closed the following month. *Author*

Right: The last 'A3' Pacific in service, No 60043 *Salmon Trout*, a classmate of the legendary *Flying Scotsman*, bursts out from beneath the London Road overbridge and past the aforementioned derailed diesel shunter. St Margaret's was unusual in having a main line running through the middle of it, separating the turntable from the running sheds. *Author*

A locomotive that needs no introduction to anyone who, like the author, had a Hornby Dublo three-rail trainset in the mid-1950s — Standard tank No 80054. Coupled up to *Salmon Trout*, the locomotive is standing on the main line, awaiting a path into St Margaret's shed yard. The building prominent in the distance is the old Munrospun woollen mill at Restalrig. *Author*

The 1965 version of the London–Edinburgh 'Flying Scotsman' (the 10am departure from King's Cross), hauled by a 'Deltic' diesel carrying that train's distinctive 'golden thistle' headboard, passes St Margaret's depot on its way to Waverley. Behind the 'V2' (No 60973) and 'B1' steam locomotives is the coaling stage, while beyond that are tenements in London Road, occupied by lucky people with a fabulous view! *Author*

Left: 'Ginger' is working his milk round in this view looking south along Bellevue Road towards Bellevue School (now Drummond Community High School) on 12 January 1985. Believe it or not there is a connection here with James Bond; actor Sean Connery, having joined St Cuthbert's Dairy at the age of 14, progressed from a barrow worker to a horseman between July 1944 and January 1950, with a short gap in between, when he joined the Royal Navy. *Peter Stubbs*

Right: With the last remnants of snowfall still evident, 24-year-old 'Ginger' tucks in to his breakfast in Bellevue Place, at the junction with Melgund Terrace, on 26 January 1985, the last day that St Cuthbert's Co-Op used horse-drawn floats to deliver milk in Edinburgh. *Peter Stubbs*

Above: No 138, one of 75 Daimler buses bought by ECT in 1949/50 but looking decidedly older, passes the stone portico of the bus station in North St Andrew Street as prospective passengers head for an inter-town service. This bus lasted in service until 1964; classmate No 135 has been preserved. *Ian Stewart*

Right: With the creation of the St James Centre office and shopping complex this view of the old St Andrew Square bus station, recorded in the summer of 1964, has changed beyond recognition. In the foreground stands No BB69, a 1949-built AEC Regent III with lowbridge Duple body, which would be withdrawn in 1966 and end up on a farmyard near Dundee. To its right, and only one year older, is No BB57, another AEC Regent III but with a lowbridge Alexander body reminiscent of wartime austerity buses. Beyond, lurking in the shadows, is Bristol FLF Lodekka AA887, new in 1962. *Maurice Bateman*

Scottish Motor Traction (SMT) was formed in 1905 to provide inter-town services and in 1936 moved its Edinburgh bus stands from Waverley Bridge to St Andrew Square, where this Bristol Lodekka, No AA13, is seen brand-new in July 1956. The Square remained the terminus for SMT (later Scottish Omnibuses) services to and from Edinburgh until the company opened St Andrew Square bus station in April 1957.
Bruce Jenkins

Bearing the short-lived 'Scottish' fleetname of the newly renamed Scottish Omnibuses is No AA18, a Bristol FS Lodekka with Eastern Coach Works body, new in 1964 when this picture was taken. The vehicle is pulling out of the bus station into North St Andrew Street. To the left, on the corner of Clyde Street, is the Travellers' Tryst bar, which was owned by Scottish<None>Omnibuses. *Maurice Bateman*

Left: St Andrew Square bus station was built alongside Clyde Street, and the Enquiries & Booking Office seen here was located on the corner of Clyde Street Lane. No A1A, an Eastern Coach Works-bodied Bristol LS coach that ran from 1954 to 1969, displays the 'EASTERN SCOTTISH' fleetname used by Scottish Omnibuses, successor to SMT. *John May*

Above: Negotiating St Andrew Square is Alexander-bodied Leyland Royal Tiger No FPC53, new in 1953 and rebuilt from centre- to front-entrance in 1965. By now the bus was operated by Alexander (Fife), one of the three companies created upon the break-up of W. Alexander & Sons in 1961. The building on the right is one of the two pavilions, designed by Robert Adam in 1769, flanking the Royal Bank of Scotland. *John May*

Left: St Andrew Square bus station is positively heaving in this view taken in July 1959. There were four platforms for local services, while tours and express services used the area just visible on the left. In 1970 an office block was built over the entrance in place of the stone portico, forming a bridge beneath which the buses had to pass. *Bruce Jenkins*

Above: City Tour coaches stand on Waverley Bridge in July 1959. In the foreground is ECT No 816, a Leyland Royal Tiger of 1952 which was converted from bus to coach in 1958 (and would be withdrawn in 1967). Behind, looking much more than just two years older, is ECT No X23, a Duple-bodied Bedford OB in its last year of service. In the background is the Old Town, including St Giles' Cathedral (on the extreme left) and the Bank of Scotland (behind the tall tree). *Bruce Jenkins*

On a private-hire duty, possibly dropping off visitors to the Ideal Home Exhibition in the Waverley Market exhibition hall (since replaced by an indoor market), Eastern Scottish Bristol LD Lodekka No AA848, built in 1961, stands on Waverley Bridge. To its rear, in Princes Street, is the R. W. Forsyth store of 1906, which was to close in 1984. *Ian Stewart*

Across the western end of Waverley station and East Princes Street Gardens in this mid-1950s view stand the base of the Scott Monument and three Princes Street landmarks of the time: The Hotel Royal, Jenners department store (still extant today) and the Old Waverley Hotel. There is considerable steam-engine activity in the platforms. Visible are a

Class V2 mixed-traffic locomotive (nearest the camera), Class A1 No 60161 *North British* (also on page 8), a streamlined Class A4 Pacific and an elderley NBR 'Scott' class. *Joseph and Richard Braun Collection/ Online Transport Archive*

When steam was axed in the 1960s in favour of diesel and electric traction, usefulness rather than age determined the order of extinction. Whereas some Victorian engines belonging to *Maude*'s class (see page 60) survived until the end of Scottish steam in 1967, locomotives built in the 1950s were lucky to see 10 years' service, and some saw considerably less. One of the last express-passenger locomotives to be built, 'Britannia' Pacific No 70052 *Firth of Tay*, was only three years old when photographed at Waverley in May 1957. *Jim Oatway*

Above right: In August 1961, with Salisbury Crags in the background, the pioneer Class A4 Pacific, No 60014 *Silver Link*, built in 1935 as LNER No 2509, completes the world's longest daily non-stop run as it brings the 'Elizabethan' express from London into the eastern end of Waverley station after a 6½-hour journey. As stated in the Introduction, a crew change was effected whilst the train was on the move. Water supplies were replenished from troughs between the rails while the train was in motion, coal supplies being just sufficient for the 393-mile journey. *Brian Patton*

Right: Another 'A4', No 60024 *Kingfisher*, prepares to leave Waverley with the afternoon 'Talisman' express to King's Cross in August 1961. The 'A4' class originally numbered 35 locomotives, but one was damaged beyond repair in an air raid on York during World War 2. Of the remainder, no fewer than six have been preserved — four in Britain and one each in Canada and the USA. *Kingfisher* was one of a handful of these magnificent machines to be retained from 1962 to 1966 for working the three-hour expresses between Glasgow and Aberdeen, this one hauling the last 'A4'-headed service on 14 September 1966.
Brian Patton

Above: The view east along Princes Street from the Scott Monument in the mid-1950s, contrasting with the westward view on page 5. On the right, beyond the Bedford coaches on the City Tour, is the flat roof of the Waverley Market, overlooked by the North British (now Balmoral) Hotel. On the left is C&A Modes' store, which burned down in 1955, next to which is R. W. Forsyth's striking edifice, with distinctive tower. Princes Street continues into Waterloo Place, with Calton Hill beyond. *Ian Stewart collection*

Back cover: At the head of two early 1920s preserved Caledonian Railway carriages carrying enthusiasts on a railtour, BR Standard Class 2 No 78046 stands at Colinton station on the Balerno line, which closed to passengers in 1943. In the background is the tunnel to which reference is made in the Introduction. The trackbed has since become a cycleway, and the tunnel is now lit. *Author's collection*